Adventures with Mr. X

An X-traordinary Rooster

Rosalind Creasy

with
Kimberly Axelrod

Copyright 2024, Rosalind Creasy
All rights reserved.

Metamorphic Press
634 Scotland Drive, Santa Rosa, CA 95409
www.robertkourik.com
rkourik@sonic.net

No part of this book may be reproduced in any form, including any mechanical means, including storage and information retrieval systems, photocopying and any electronic means, without the written consent of the author. The information in this book is true and complete to the best of the author's knowledge. All recommendations are made without guarantees on the part of the author. The author and publisher disclaim any and all liability incurred because of the use of the information contained in this book.

ISBN: 978-0-9615848-5-6

Library of Congress Control Number: 2024914457

Chelsea Green Publishing, Inc.
Distributed in North America by:
Chelsea Green Publishing
White River Junction, Vermont, USA
London, UK
www.chelseagreen.com
All wholesale and retail sales by Chelsea Green
My website sales at www.robertkourik.com

Cover: Mr. X
A Golden Duckwing Standard Old English Game Fowl, one of the oldest chicken breeds in the world.

Front and back cover photos © Rosalind Creasy, 2024

Printed in the United States of America, *not* China. Cruelty-free, not tested on animals.
Vegan paper. Caffeine free. No GMOs, Recyclable. Totally groovy.

10 9 8 7 6 5 4 3 2 1

Dedicated to:

Robert Creasy:
To the love of my life
and adventurer extraordinaire

Acknowledgments

I want to express my deep appreciation to the many people who made this book a fitting tribute to my husband Robert and to the inimitable Mr. X.

My books have never been a solitary venture, but documenting this story and making sense out of nearly 30-year-old records was the most challenging task I've ever attempted—it truly did take a village. (It was also a bit like assembling a 2,000-piece jigsaw puzzle; where do you even start?) This is where Kim Axelrod deserves the highest praise! Her capacity to organize information is truly without parallel. Without her help and that of her husband Steve Axelrod on tech support, this book would not have been possible.

I want to also thank my immediate family, starting with my grandson, Alex Chavarin, who helped with the initial organization and more tech support. At the beginning of this project, the two of us spent hours of "quality time" searching though files and photos and jotting information on countless descriptive Post-it™ notes that we dated and plastered around the guestroom walls.

Thanks also to my immediate family, Laura and Joel Chavarin and Bob and Julie Creasy, for their many hours of reminiscing about their years of interacting with Mr. X, and for their valuable feedback. I also want to appreciate Gail and Bill Gammerdinger and other family members who provided photos and background information.

My long-time friend Marcie Hawthorne, who spent many hours with Mr. X, also gave invaluable feedback and helped flesh out this story, as did my neighbors Kris and Bob Stanfield and Katie Bodkin. Thanks also to my gardeners—Rayne MacGeorge, Jody Main, and Deborah Stern—who not only kept my garden healthy and productive, but often provided care for our beloved fowl.

And many thanks go to the people who brought this book to production. They include my editors, Kathy Barash and Amie Hill, for help in refining the story, and Patty Buttitta, of Buttitta Design, for her marvelous cover visuals.

Much credit also goes to Robert Kourik, of Metamorphic Press. His coordination and layout design skills brought this complex project together and made the stories come to life. For more information on Robert, visit: www.robertkourik.com.

For more information about Rosalind and updates to Mr. X's life, visit Rosalind's web page: www.rosalindcreasy.com

 # Table of Contents

Chapter 1   In the Beginning....................................... 1

Chapter 2   Off to College - Felton, CA..................... 11

Chapter 3   Settling Back in at Home........................15

Chapter 4   The Adventure Begins.............................25

Chapter 5   Teppanyaki - Hillburn, New York.........35

Chapter 6   Go with the Flo - Honesdale, PA...........39

Chapter 7   New York City, New York.........................43

Chapter 8   Long Island and Beyond.........................49

Chapter 9   Florida Reunion.......................................57

Chapter 10   Home at Last...63

Chapter 11   Albuquerque, New Mexico....................67

Chapter 12   An Unexpected Goodbye......................71

Chapter 13   A Birthday Bash......................................75

Chapter 14   Mr. X Takes a Bath..................................81

Chapter 15   Slowing Down...85

Chapter 16   Crossing the Rainbow Bridge...............91

Epilogue 95

Chapter 1

In the Beginning - 1995

Mr. X didn't like cold French fries—only warm ones.

Why, you ask, would a rooster eat French fries—warm or cold?

Well, the answer is: When my late husband, Robert, and Mr. X traveled across the United States in 2001, they were forced to eat at drive-throughs because you certainly can't bring a rooster inside a restaurant.

So, now you are asking yourself, why would anyone be driving in a car with a rooster, much less making a trek across America with a chicken as a companion?

That's another good question, so let me start at the beginning.

Okay, be prepared to fall in love with a rooster. Thousands of people across America have. Certainly Robert and I did.

To be clear, neither of us ever expected to fall in love with a chicken of any description. That's crazy! Sure, a dog or cat, even a guinea pig or hamster—but a rooster? Ridiculous! And why would large numbers of other people go gaga over the same feisty fowl?

Here's an example: after experiencing a few drive-in restaurants on that cross-country trip with Robert, Mr. X somehow learned that an order-stand meant that treats were in the offing, and, as Robert would pull up to the service window, the intelligent bird would start to chortle and cluck loudly.

The folks working behind the window could often hear Mr. X voicing his anticipatory appreciation, and usually, by the time Robert's car pulled up to it, a server or two would be leaning out, looking for the source of this strange noise.

In every case they would ask, "Is that a rooster?" At Robert's nod, they would inevitably ask: "Can we see him?" If nobody was in line behind him, Robert would pull over and take Mr. X over to the window so they could admire him. This was a foretaste of the joy, delight, and smiles Mr. X would leave behind him wherever he went.

In case you're wondering, this is the tale of how we became rooster parents.

In 1995, Robert and I were visiting friends Patty and Milt Clauser at their ranch in Albuquerque, New Mexico, and for breakfast they served us delicious eggs that had been laid by their extensive flock of hens. This gave Robert an idea: why not take two fertile eggs, package them for our flight home to California, and try to hatch them?

The timing seemed perfect. As a newly retired computer scientist, Robert now had time to raise a few chicks, and I—a garden designer, photographer, and author known for celebrating, designing, and writing about the concept known as "Edible Landscaping" had long wanted to have chickens in my garden to eat pests and provide delicious, fresh eggs.

Once we were home, Robert, ever the scientist, did his homework. He found detailed information on hatching chickens in *The Chicken Health Handbook*, by Gail Damerow. (All right, this may be more information than you think you need or want, but please bear with me, as I want to give you an idea both of how detail-oriented Robert was, and also to provide some helpful hints in case you want to raise chickens yourself.)

According to Robert's research, in order to start the process, you need the optimum temperature to hatch fertile eggs, combined with the recommended humidity for the incubator. In addition, it's critical to rotate (turn the eggs over) every eight hours. You're acting as the surrogate mama hen who carefully turns the eggs over three or four times a day to make sure that the developing chicks won't stick to the shell.

Robert chose a large cardboard box for the hatching process, and set up a thermometer and humidity-gauge to provide ideal conditions. For warmth, he used a clip-on light with an incandescent bulb. He then set the box on our kitchen table, made a nest in a pie-pan lined with paper from his shredder, and surrounded it with wood shavings.

Before he put the eggs in the box, Robert used a Sharpie™ to mark a small X on the side of one egg and an O on the other, so he could tell them apart and properly rotate them. He then declared that X would be called "Kiss," and O was "Hug." We now had to wait 21 days to see if all of this would produce actual chickens.

Two weeks into this adventure, my mother visited from Florida, and we decided to drive 350 miles to Altadena, California, to visit our daughter, Laura, her husband, Joel, and my grandson Alex. We figured that the eggs, now 16 days into their incubation, would hatch while we were there.

Robert prided himself on being a car-packing wizard, and he somehow fit all of our luggage, the incubator, and some necessary baby-chick supplies into our compact Honda. He decided that our Coleman™ cooler would work better than cardboard for a nesting box, because it was more portable and would better maintain the temperature and humidity. So off we went: Robert and I in the front seats and Mom in the back, keeping a wary eye on the cooler.

Once we arrived at Laura and Joel's, Robert set up the incubator in a safe spot, but after a few hours in Altadena's arid climate, he concluded that its humidity was too low. To add moisture,

Who knew that you could use an old cooler to incubate eggs.

In the Beginning 3

Nice and cozy - the heat and humidity were just right.

he created a wick with an old piece of dishtowel, placed one end of it in a jar of water inside the cooler, and hung the other end outside the cooler. He then resumed the routine of checking and adjusting the humidity and turning the eggs.

Finally, on September 30th at approximately 7:00 a.m.—21 days after incubation—a tiny hole (known as a "pip") appeared on the "Kiss" egg! We watched this development with eager excitement.

Hatching is quite a workout for the emerging chick. After the first pip, the chick uses an "egg tooth" to chip away one tiny piece of shell at a time until it has circumnavigated most of the shell. This is exhausting for such a small creature but necessary; it helps to strengthen and align its legs. Since chicks are forced to rest in between chips, the process usually takes at least 24 hours.

We estimated that the egg finally hatched around 4:00 a.m. on October 1st. Looking back, I realize that the emergence of chick from egg is such a simple event that plays out all over the planet every day, yet seeing it in person was amazing, evoking such a feeling of wonder and joy! This wet and weary little critter was now part of our lives.

Look out world, here I come.

We eagerly watched the "Hug" egg for signs of activity, but nothing happened. After a few hours, Robert held the egg up to a strong lightbulb, revealing a dark mass inside, but no sign of movement. The next day we sadly buried Hug's egg in the back garden.

More about chicks from Gail Damerow again?: "Imprinting is a form of learning in which an animal gains its sense of species identification. Birds don't automatically know what they are when they hatch—they visually imprint on their parents during an early critical period of development. After imprinting, they will identify with

In the Begining 5

Look at me all downy and cute.

that species for life… if young birds imprint on humans, they will identify with humans rather than their own species." Little did we know at the time that Kiss was imprinting on all of the humans gathered around to watch our baby bird try to figure out which way was up.

Before long, the little chick's down was dry and fluffy, and Robert took an official photo to send to friends. What a cutie! Needless to say, this wee fluffball was the center of attention for the rest of our visit. (My mom confessed later that she was a bit miffed because she was used to occupying that role when we visited.)

Our visit over, we loaded everything up and headed for home. Once there, Robert returned Kiss to the climate-controlled box, and the care and feeding continued.

As the chick grew stronger, Robert took Kiss outside regularly for fun-and-socialization time. Every day, the little bird grew larger, with new feathers appearing daily. Somehow I was convinced that we had a cute little hen. In anticipation, I did some research to determine when she might lay her first egg. The books said 18 weeks—maybe for Valentine's Day?

Kiss was about six weeks old when Robert decided to take a trip to Los Angeles, leaving me as surrogate Mother Hen. He moved the cardboard box into my office and set it on a table near my computer, and it was a delight to hear my feath-

Fun in the sun on Robert's knee.

Kiss sharing the attention with Daniel the cat.

In the Beginning 7

ery companion chirping along to my music as I wrote. Then, on November 18th, I happened to be talking to my husband on the phone when suddenly I heard a very feeble, "Ca..ca.... caaa...cooo.. cooockadoodledoo."

"Congratulations," I said to Robert. "It's a boy!"

For almost four months, day after day, Robert routinely took Kiss out to the back garden for together time. It wasn't long before Daniel Boone's Farm, a female cat, joined the spontaneous men's group. By then it was fall; as the weather started to get colder, our rooster acquired many more feathers and was becoming quite handsome.

We had assumed that he would be a brown-hued Araucana, as Patty's flock was comprised mostly of that breed. Much to our surprise, Kiss's new feathers came in different shades of white, brown, yellow, and iridescent blue. (As I was doing some research for this book I learned that he was in fact a Golden Duckwing Standard Old English Game fowl, but more about that later.)

Along with feathers, he began to develop some seriously cocky attitude. Robert decided the girly name "Kiss" no longer fit his macho guy, and declared that our rooster would henceforth be known as "Mr. X."

At first a bit of a mongrel, now a magnificent beast.

8 In the Begining

It may be beautiful, but where are the delicious slugs?

Chapter 2

Off to College - Felton, California - 1996

On February 23rd, 1996, when Mr. X was 21 weeks old, things changed suddenly for us as rooster parents. That was day that our adventurous bird suddenly decided to fly to the top of —and over—the neighbors' fence. Witnessing this, Robert hurried around to find the feathered fugitive already chowing down on a bed of prized flowers.

Since general chicken husbandry, as opposed to keeping a rooster as a house-and-yard-pet, wasn't then part of our lifestyle, we came to the reluctant conclusion that we had to find our beloved rooster a new home.

Renee Shepherd, a long-time friend (well-known for her company Renee's Garden Seeds),

After roughing up the resident rooster, Mr. X now resides with a black pygmy goat.

suggested that an animal-loving friend and neighbor of hers, Glenna Von Geas, might adopt him. Glenna lived in Felton, about half an hour away, and we made an appointment with her to check out Mr. X's possible new home.

Glenna lived on a small ranch pleasantly set among redwoods, where she tended a number of rescued animals. Near the house were two relatively small coops, one containing a rooster and another a pygmy black goat. While Felton was farther away than we preferred, it seemed to be the best solution, so a few weeks later, we sadly loaded Mr. X into a dog carrier and drove him off to Glenna's. When friends inquired

Glenna admires her newest rooster.

Together again, Robert and M. X.

Tom and Will Gammerdinger compete to see whose arm he will choose.

Mom needed her sunglasses because his plumage was so bright.

12 Off to College

where he'd gone Robert told them that we'd "sent him off to college."

Soon after we arrived at Glenna's, Mr. X encountered his first away-from-home challenge. Logic seemed to dictate that he should go in the coop with the other rooster. Because our boy had never seen another chicken before, and seemed to think of himself as human, we naturally wondered what he would do.

Well, to our chagrin and embarrassment, his rooster instincts kicked in immediately; he attacked his new "roommate," knocked him over, and pinned him to the ground! After this happened a few more times, it seemed clear that Mr. X belonged in the coop with the pygmy goat, who seemed calmly indifferent to this arrangement. That transfer was peaceful, and after reviewing our boy's idiosyncrasies and favorite foods with Glenna, we said our sad goodbyes.

After a few short weeks without our pet, we just had to visit him. The big question was: would he recognize us? Silly question; the moment Mr. X spotted us walking up the long driveway, he literally exploded with excitement, greeting us with an exuberant dance and a stream of fond cockadoodleing. Oh my, he was so thrilled! He immediately flew onto Robert's arm and kept on crowing and crowing. We decided that we needed to visit more often.

In the meantime, Glenna had learned that she could let him out to wander around when she was gardening and feeding the other animals. She also could carry him around and give him treats. Unlike her other rooster, Mr. X would come out when invited and obediently come in when she asked him, so eventually she let him out to explore and scratch for bugs during much of the day. For almost five years we would visit Mr. X. Sometimes I went when I had business with Renee, other times we took visiting friends and relatives, and there were times that we just missed him. Each time we went through the same ritual. Mr. X would recognize our car, dance around and greet us with much crowing as we walked up the driveway, and each time we left he would call out a long mournful cockadoodledoo.

About four years into his Felton residence, Mr. X had a close brush with death. Glenna said he was out foraging when a coyote showed up. Unfortunately the coop door had not been closed tightly and the coyote was able to push the door open and kill the other rooster. Glenna heard all the squawking and came running out, only to see the carnage. She called and looked and didn't see Mr. X. She scared off the coyote with a broom and then searched in dread, fearing that he had been carried off and she would have to call with the bad news. Finally, he popped his head out of her abandoned pickup truck's window. Apparently, Mr. X had seen the coyote and flown up and into the truck's open window! That was a harrowing adventure.

Another year or so went by, but then, on a visit to see Mr. X, Glenna gave us the sad news that she was ill and needed to find homes for her animals. It was time to take Mr. X home.

Chapter 3

Settling Back in at Home

What a joy to get our "boy" home! The feeling seemed to be mutual; as soon as we pulled into the driveway Mr. X began to chortle happily. Within seconds of hopping out of the car, he plucked a slug out of the boxwood and gobbled it up greedily, following his snack with a formidable "cock-a-doodle-doo!" obviously proclaiming: "Listen up y'all, I'm in charge here!"

We let him explore a little more as we emptied the car, and when Robert opened up the garage door, Mr. X walked right in, waited while Robert filled his food bowl, and then tucked in like a champ. Appetite satisfied, he let out another classic crow that clearly said: "I'm home!"

I still remember how, a few days later, I happened to look into the living room, and there was Robert in his favorite chair, with Mr. X cuddled on his lap, both guys blissfully watching car racing. In deference to my no-chickens-in-the-house rule, Robert had set his feathered pal on a large rag in case of accidents. When he saw me, my husband looked up rather sheepishly and said, "I didn't realize how much I missed him." I felt the same way.

Having learned our lesson about the perils of keeping Mr. X as a free-range fowl, we now realized that we needed a chicken coop; but where to put it? Roosters are loud—REALLY loud—and not just in the morning. In reality, it's anytime they hear a disturbance or sense

Hi world, I'm baaack.

a threat. A rooster's role is to be the early-warning system and proud protector of his flock. Anything—a wandering skunk, barking dog, owl circling nearby, an unwary mail carrier—will set a rooster off, anytime, day or night.

Tradition dictates that a chicken coop be built in the backyard, and just about any book or internet source about home chicken coops assumes this is what you want to do. We reasoned, however, that our neighborhood of quarter-acre lots meant that any backyard coop would be too near our neighbors' (not to mention our) bedrooms.

My front yard coop.

After checking with folks living nearby, we decided to go against protocol and zoning laws and build the coop in our front yard about 15 feet back from the street and under a cedar tree for shade. (The green coop is behind the wooden picket fence in the upper right corner of the photograph above.) This turned out to be a fabulous decision! Not only was it quieter, but the excitement, amusement, and joy that our accessible coop has given countless neighbors for 25 years has enriched so many lives.

Generations of neighborhood children have gotten to know and enjoy our fascinating feathered critters over the years. I grow sorrel, a hardy perennial that chickens love, near the curb and the kids eagerly pick off leaves to shove through the chicken wire and watch the new hens cluck and dance around enjoying their treat.

Eventually I ran into our mayor, with whom I'd

Dagan kickin' back and getting his sorrel ready for the flock.

worked over the years. I was a little nervous about our situation vis-à-vis local regulations, but she just winked and asked me how my rooster was doing, assuring me that: "If the neighbors don't mind, why should the city?"

There were two unintended consequences, however, of having a rooster in a front-yard coop. Our great neighbors the Stanfields had a parakeet that started to imitate the cock-a-doodling; this understandably got on their nerves from time to time. And then there was the time that Mr. X made the Police Blotter in our local paper, *The Town Crier*!

"Disturbance: A loud rooster was reported at 5:59 a.m. Wednesday—three minutes after sunrise." What happened? There were new neighbors renting the house across the street with two teenaged daughters. It was a hot night and the girls' room was in the front of the house; most likely their windows were open. It turned out that we'd forgotten to close the garage door (At night, because of his natural inspiration to serenade the sunrise, Mr. X bunked in a large dog carrier in the garage). Clearly, because of their natural inspiration to sleep in, the teens had reported it to the police! Oh well…

Once we had the coop built, we established a daily

The new hens arrive in their "girly" travel box.

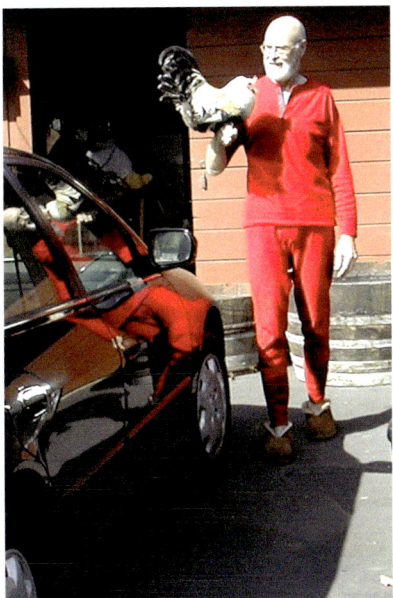

Robert performs the morning ritual to the coop in his signature red jammies.

routine. Mid-morning, one of us would either carry him from the garage to the coop or let him walk over and hop in. In the early evening, we reversed the routine.

It wasn't too long before we figured that, since we had a coop, we might as well get some hens. (Hooray—fresh eggs!) Robert decided that this would be a good excuse to revisit Patty and Milt in Albuquerque and acquire four hens of egg-bearing age to co-habit with Mr. X.

At the ranch, with much scrutiny, Robert chose four likely females from the large roaming flock. After a few days of feeding, petting, and otherwise socializing them, he put them into a large cardboard box and loaded them into the car. Since he didn't want to have to deal with staying overnight somewhere with a boxful of chickens, he decided to drive 15 hours straight to get home.

This turned out, of course, to be more difficult than he had anticipated. He was stopped at the California border to make sure he wasn't bringing in anything illegal, and an

Settling Back in at Home 17

officious inspector insisted that Robert open the box so he could see what was inside.

Of course, as soon as the container was opened, the four hens immediately rocketed out, squawking, and scattered all over the inside of the car! Robert had to pull off the road and spend a good 15 minutes catching the panicked birds and stuffing them back into their box. It was a circus! As soon as he'd get one hen in the box, another would jump out, et cetera, et cetera. What a squawking mess—feathers and poop all over him and the car!

Robert and the girls, all somewhat the worse for wear, arrived home fairly early in the morning. Since Mr. X was still in the garage, Robert put the hens in their new home and gave them a few hours to get settled in.

By this time, the routine of bringing Mr. X into the garage at night and taking him out in the morning had become the norm. Sometimes during the day, I allowed him to wander around the garden with me. Early on, I discovered that he had an eagle eye for pesky critters, including those garden menaces, slugs and earwigs, which he devoured with a loud greedy chortle. He was an easy companion who stayed by my side or nearby, and was fun to watch as he stalked around happily foraging for bugs. Although sometimes he'd help himself to some lettuce or a ripe strawberry, it was absolutely worth it!

Since a rooster in the front yard is not a common suburban sight, we had a few unusual adventures. One day, while he was out foraging with me, a FedEx delivery woman came hurrying up the front walk. Mr. X, startled, promptly flew up in her face and attacked her. (Because he often treated me as one of his flock I presume he thought he was protecting me.) After that inci-

Showing off in the garden.

dent, I began picking up my packages at the FedEx office. The employees always acknowledged me with a smile, announcing: "The Rooster Lady is here!"

Another garden adventure, part of which I was able to capture on film, occurred on one of the occasions when our neighbor's cat, Pretty Kitty, came over to cheekily put her paw through the chicken-wire of the pen and taunt Mr. X. He always responded by trying to peck her paw.

One day Mr. X was out in the garden and Pretty Kitty came sneaking up behind him. What she didn't know was that chickens have a 300-degree field of vision—he certainly saw her, but on this occasion acted as if he didn't. He walked over to one of my planting beds; she continued slinking around behind him, then moved in front of him. He didn't budge, although I noticed that he was giving her the classic stink-eye. Finally, she reached a paw out to touch his beak, and he still didn't move!

I thought to myself: "This is going to be exciting; he's going to explode in her face!" I readied my camera. The cat's paw got within an inch of the rooster's beak and suddenly she seemed to catch on that he was not one bit scared. I could almost see her register the realization: "Yikes! He might beat me up!" and she took off like a rocket. I'd been waiting anxiously to catch the big ruckus on film, but within a few seconds she was out of there. She moved so fast that I missed that particular photo, but Mr. X sure got his message across: "Mess with me at your peril!"

So this is one of the main lessons we all learned from Mr. X: You are what and who you think you are! Mr. X, in his own roosterly opinion, was pure Alpha! As you'll see, in his adventures all over the country, wherever he went, this bird didn't just own his own space, he dominated it, exuding confidence. How to describe this mindset in words? Chutzpah comes

Settling Back in at Home 19

to mind first, then (appropriately) "Cocky," and (definitely) "I'm In Charge here!" I like to think that he saw himself as "The Rock"—the Dwayne Johnson-action-hero of the rooster world!

This attitude soon became a central fact of our lives, as Robert and I then traveled a lot, both for business and pleasure, and delegating care of Mr. X while we were out of town became a challenge. Although I've mentioned how feisty he could be, generally Mr. X was a mellow fellow outside of the coop—except when an unknown person showed up in his territory; then he was quick to defend his hens or his human "flock." When my family or our gardener entered, he was fine, but any new caretaker had to be on guard.

Because of this, we decided to see how well he could travel, so we could bring him along on some of our trips. With that in mind, we planned a trial journey to visit long-time friends, Marcie (below) and Dan Hawthorne, at their ranch in San Luis Obispo, in southern California. Our son, Bob, and his wife, Julie, drove down, too, accompanied by Hope, their black standard poodle.

Now, you may be wondering: "What about the hens?" Well, the hens were basically low-maintenance, living in their coop 24/7. Although they had to be fed and watered, and the coop kept clean, any willing friend or neighbor could do that. The hens basically didn't react any differently to other people than they did to Robert and me. Compared to Mr. X, their personalities were black and white, while he was vivid, living Technicolor™! People were happy to volunteer to take care of the hens in exchange for free eggs.

For our trip, Robert packed Mr. X's cage in the

Marcie Hawthorne enjoying time in her garden with Mr. X.

20 Settling Back in at Home

backseat along with all his food, bedding, and our luggage, and off we went. As it turned out, our rooster was a helpful driving companion, letting the driver know every time a truck was about to pass us by giving out a small chirp as it approached.
After a few hours, we stopped for a quick, fast-food lunch (which was how Mr. X first developed a taste for warm French fries). As soon as we arrived at the ranch, our guy immediately hopped out and started to let everyone know that he was, "large and in charge" by puffing up and letting out some very loud cock-a-doodles— almost as if he were saying, "I'm here! Bring it on!"

Robert carried the bird to an enclosed courtyard, and we all got settled in. Mr. X liked his new environment, chortling as he explored and rooted around to find countless new hiding spots with edible critters.

Later, all of us, including Mr. X and Hope the poodle, gathered on the back deck to enjoy the sunset. Mr. X immediately decided that Hope should only be allowed on the far side of the deck, away from the gathering. Every time she tried to join our group, Mr. X would head her off. Finally, to keep peace in the family, Robert put the fierce fowl back in his crate for the evening.

The next afternoon, while hanging out in the courtyard, we discovered a new side of Mr. X's character. Robert wore the distinctive boots from L.L.Bean and Mr. X would attack them when ever he saw them left somewhere. He also got excited at the sight of red painted toenails! Let's face it, the dude had an obsession.

Settling Back in at Home 21

Mr. X attacks Robert's shoes with enthusiasm.

22 Settling Back in at Home

Mr . X especially liked Robert's Bean boots from LL Bean.

Chapter 4

The Adventure Begins

After we returned home, Robert decided that Mr. X would be a fine companion for a long-anticipated cross-country trip.

Now that he was retired, Robert had time to travel and to visit many of his relatives, his friends from work, and other people he'd met while scuba diving. During his college years, Robert had learned this pursuit from none other than Jacques Cousteau, the co-inventor of underwater diving gear and producer/host/star of dozens of underwater-themed TV shows. Scuba diving was one of Robert's passions, and he had made many friends on his numerous dive trips.

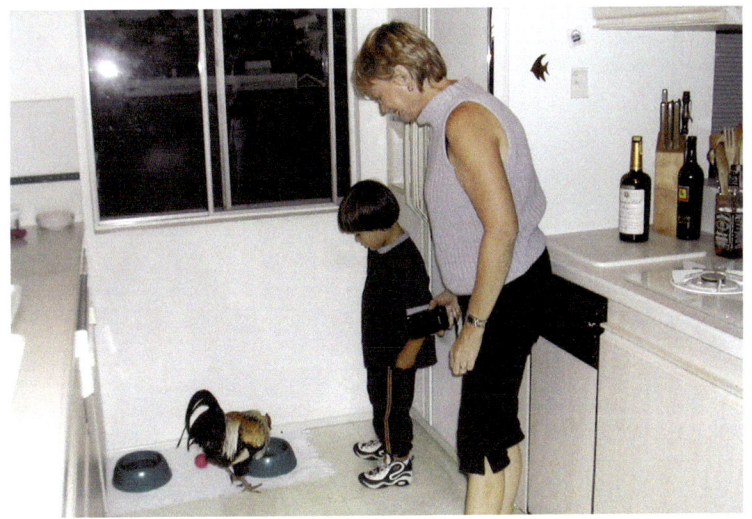

Linda Avery and Alex watch on as Mr. X enjoys his supper.

I, on the other hand, though I would have liked to accompany him on the initial phase of this odyssey, had to stay home and work on a manuscript for a magazine article, so I made plans to join him in New York City mid-journey and then we'd continue together.

That August, Robert started contacting people to make his plans. He concluded that having Mr. X along would make it a lot more fun, and in that notion, he turned out to be more than correct.

My husband kicked off his adventure in Los Angeles, and stayed with our daughter, Laura, her husband, Joel, and grandson, Alex, for a few days. While he was there, he visited with Linda and Pete Avery, scuba pals living nearby in Manhattan Beach.

On a whim, they decided it would be fun to take Mr. X to see the ocean, and watch his reaction to its rolling immensity. First question was what would he do? Would he be afraid of the roaring surf? What if he wanted to go in the water. I remember one of us asking if chickens can swim? (The answer to that I recently found out is yes they can swim for a short time but if they are in the water very long their feathers soak up too much water and they will sink and can drown. They are also prone to hyperthermia if the water is cold and their feathers get saturated.)

Mr X rooting around for a new found delicacy sand crabs.

Robert proudly showing off his buddy Mr. X.

26 The Adventure Begins

Pete Avery enjoys Mr. X as we stand for the family portrait.

Not only was he not intimidated, He headed straight for the tidal area and immediately started rooting around and soon discovered that sand crabs were delicious! He went from one little burrow to the next. I bet he ate at least a half dozen. To document the event we took a family portrait. He had a wonderful time, as did the many people who gathered to watch him—including the lifeguard on duty. I'm sure that they couldn't wait to tell their friends what they had seen on the beach. Too bad that there were no smartphones back then!

After their beach idyll, Robert and Mr. X headed east, to the plains city of Alpine, Texas. Although perfectly aware that he couldn't stay in a regular hotel or motel when accompanied by a rooster, Robert knew from previous trips that the rental cabins at a place called the Antelope Lodge were located far enough apart so that Mr. X's dawn serenades wouldn't wake the other guests.

This was Robert's first real test of traveling with a rooster, and they soon established a routine: Robert would bring Mr. X's dog crate into his room, lay down newspapers to catch poop, and put his companion's water and food in the shower.

Although chickens are pretty much impossible to housebreak and usually poop every 30 minutes, amazingly Mr. X never once pooped on anyone! Anybody holding him learned that if he wiggled a lot, that was the signal to put him down somewhere where he could do his business.

Mr. X looks over the cabin where Robert laid down towels and newspaper on the floor.

On their first morning at the Lodge, Robert let Mr. X out to get some exercise and scratch for edible bugs and worms. And wouldn't you know it, our stalwart bird's first encounter was with one of the few creatures that he instinctively knew he couldn't dominate—a mother peahen and her young. Do not mess with Motherhood! He carefully tiptoed off to forage elsewhere.

The city of Alpine, located in the Big Bend area of Texas, is 15 minutes or so from Marfa, home of the mysterious "Marfa Lights." For generations, from the times of early Native American settlements to the present day, residents have occasionally seen a series of dancing lights flickering over the Marfa Plains.

From Wikipedia: "The Marfa lights, also known as the Marfa ghost lights, have been observed near U.S. Route 67 on Mitchell Flat east of Marfa, Texas, in the United States. They have gained some fame as onlookers have attributed them to paranormal phenomena such as ghosts, UFOs, or a will-o'-the-wisp."

Robert, who had a degree in physics, had long been interested in all sorts of unexplained phenomena. He and a college buddy, Ed Hendricks, had visited Marfa on numerous occasions, using different instruments in attempts to determine the origin of the odd illuminations.

Even though they had seen the lights quite a few times, they were far from solving the puzzle. When Robert was there before—often for a

28 The Adventure Begins

An imposing mother peahen and her chicks.

The Marfa Lights historical marker in Marfa, Texas.

week at a time—he had made a few local friends and visited the Apache Trading Post from time to time. This time, he and Mr. X even got to know a few of the resident donkeys.

As it happened, Robert was in Marfa on the morning of September 11th, 2001. He called to tell me to turn on the TV to see the catastrophe that was happening in New York City. Like many other Americans, we were horrified, but I also had another concern: I was scheduled to fly into NYC to meet with one of my editors within the week, and also had commitments to give two lectures in New York. The questions then became: first, would my flight be canceled, and second, did I want to fly at all?

I made the decision to go, because I concluded, wrongly or rightly, that this might be the safest time to fly, as everyone in the airline industry would be super tuned in. My flight

The Adventure Begins 29

Robert and Mr. X pose with the donkeys.

was only about a third full, and before we took off, the crew came back and thanked us for being there and trusting them to keep us safe.

Robert decided that the best thing that he could do was to continue his journey, allowing Mr. X to charm people and make them smile through those anxious times. They spent a week in Alpine, and although they'd failed to solve the mystery of the lights, it was time to leave. Before his departure, Robert used bleach to sterilize the shower, and made sure he left his cabin without a single trace of a rooster.

Their next destination was Kerrville, in the middle of Texas, to visit an old work and scuba-diving buddy, Pat Crisman. Pat lived alone and was about to have hip surgery. Robert was able to bring her home from the hospital, act as her caretaker, and help with her cats during the first week of her recovery. Said felines were, needless to say, left with a healthy respect for roosters.

Once Pat was sufficiently on the mend, it was time for Robert to head east to Honesdale, Pennsylvania, to visit his beloved Aunt Flo. As it was going to be a long drive, he purchased a piece of cholla cactuswood for Mr. X to perch on. He attached this makeshift chicken-seat to the open door of the glove compartment with a bungee cord, and at last Mr. X could see out the front windshield, which made him one happy rooster.

Pat Crisman's cat gives Mr. X a wide berth.

30 The Adventure Begins

Mr. X prepares to get on the cholla cactus perch Robert attached to the glove compartment door.

He spent long hours happily taking in and commenting on the scenery.

I don't have a record of this part or Robert's itinerary, but I know that he occasionally took photos of sights along the way such as the "World's Largest Roadrunner, Paisano Pete."

From the Fort Stockton Pioneer newspaper: "Pete" was the brainchild of Fort Stockton Mayor Gene Cummings. Set at mid-stride, as if about to take off wildly across West Texas, this feathered friend has been the adopted symbol of the community ever since his creation, appearing on signs throughout town, and even getting nicely dressed up for Christmas! (Robert somehow failed to note Mr. X's reaction to this enormous fowl.)

The traveling buddies fell into a routine, using highway rest areas to stretch their legs and give Mr. X a chance to check out the local bug populations. Robert located lodgings with strategically private cabins, and stopped only at drive-through restaurants. As mentioned, they stopped at so many drive-throughs that Mr. X invariably got really excited when he realized that they were approaching an order stand. His loud chortling and trills, audible for some distance, usually resulted in smiling people leaning out of the order window to discover their source.

If there was no one behind him in line, Robert would take Mr. X out and bring him over to the window so they could see him up close and make a fuss over him and rush to bring his order of French fries. This interaction was exciting for the crews; after all, few of them had ever seen a rooster up close, much less such a gorgeous one.

The Adventure Begins

Mr. X admires the Paisano Pete statue.

Robert sits back to relax at the Alpine Lodge while Mr. X forages for critters .

32 The Adventure Begins

Mr. X looks around at a roadside rest stop.

Chapter 5

Teppanyaki - Hillburn, New York

The trip to Pennsylvania was otherwise uneventful, and Robert and his wingman arrived at Robert's Aunt Flo's house on September 22nd. Flo was delighted to see her "Bobbie," and utterly charmed to meet Mr. X.

The next day, Robert and Mr. X picked me up at JFK Airport. My plane landed safely, and Robert arrived at the airport with a hamburger for me, and a McSalad™ for our boy, with whom I had an enthusiastic reunion.

After my meeting in New York City, we decided, on a whim, to drive about an hour north to the place where Robert and I had spent our honeymoon forty years earlier— the "Motel on the Mountain" in Hillburn, NY.

We found the right spot on the mountain, but instead of the expected motel, there was now a Japanese "Teppanyaki" restaurant. Teppanyaki is a post-World War II style of Japanese cuisine that uses a propane-heated, flat-surfaced, iron griddle to cook food. (A "teppan" is the flat metal cooking surface and "yaki" means grilled, broiled, or pan-fried.)

For our version of old times' sake, we decided to eat there. It had a fairly small and isolated parking lot, so we felt it would be safe to leave Mr. X in the car. Inside there were only four other diners, at a table that seated 12, all about half our age. A courting couple and two young men who were having a joyous reunion.

At the airport Mr. X contemplates his lunch - a McSalad.

Although there were many others in the restaurant. We were quickly seated at a large table fitted out with a grill. The chef came to our grill table, and started cooking one seafood delicacy after another. Meanwhile, the other couples were busy chatting among themselves at the same counter, but by the time the main course was served, we had become part of the conversation. They told us a little about themselves and, of course, Robert started telling them about our marvelous adventure.

We all looked on in anticipation as our talented chef started grilling our dinner.

When he got to the part where we were traveling with our rooster, you could almost see them roll their eyes. And of course, nearly in unison, they all exclaimed: "ROOOOOSSTER!?" I'm sure they thought that these old folks (we were 60 at the time) were delusional, and they challenged Robert to prove it. "Okay," we said with cheerful anticipation, "When we leave we'll show you."

After we paid our tab, Robert went to the parking lot and collected Mr. X. Our dining companions were gobsmacked, shaking their heads in disbelief, wanting to touch him and pet him and learn more about our adventures.

Just then, a Mexican family drove up, all wearing festive costumes. An elderly gentleman, the grandfather, spotted Mr. X, and, unable to restrain himself, asked to hold him. Within seconds, the old man had started to quietly weep, telling us: "I grew up on a farm with a pet rooster and I haven't held one since!" Oh, how I wish I could have taken a picture of him in his beautiful black sombrero, tears running down his face, tenderly holding Mr. X, who nestled quietly in his arms as if aware that this was a special moment.

We left the restaurant and found lodging in a nearby town. Because it wasn't possible to take Mr. X in with us, we crossed our fingers and decided to leave him in the car, parked far enough away to not disturb the other guests.

After his loud dawn crowing, Mr. X always stayed the night in the car.

Chapter 6

Go with the Flo - Honesdale, PA

On September 24th, we arrived back at Flo's. We settled in and Robert rooster-proofed the yard. He put out a crossing sign to warn her many visitors of Mr. X's grazing.

Mr. X taking in all of the gloriousness of Pennsylvania.

This was also a time for some rooster grooming. Just like our fingernails, rooster's beaks and spurs keep growing their entire life unless they are ground down naturally from wear and tear. Usually this is not a problem, but when handling him Robert preferred to keep them trimmed and because they were around a lot of people he thought it was prudent. By this time, Robert thought Mr. X's spurs and beak had gotten a bit long and needed some trimming so he used a file that Flo had on hand for his spurs and used nail clippers on his beak because the upper part was sticking out a bit more than normal.

Go with the Flo 39

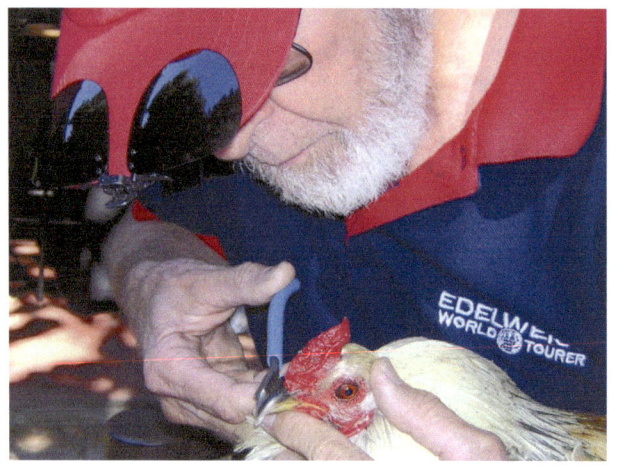

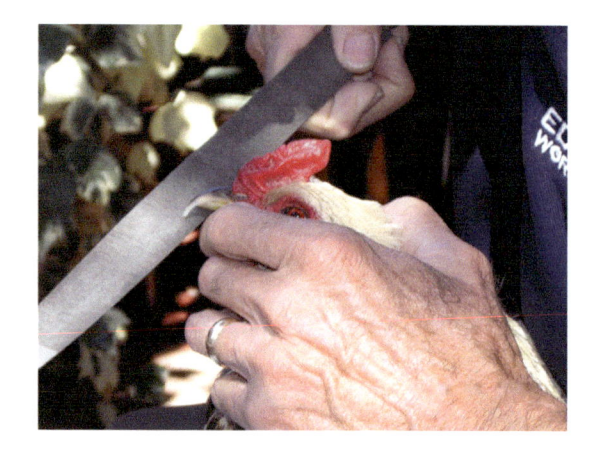

Robert carefully clipped his overgrown beak and then smoothed it with a file.

The first night, Robert put Mr. X's kennel in a far back bedroom, but that didn't go well. Even far from us, his morning crowing woke us all up. For the rest of the visit, we moved the kennel back to the car for the night.

The next day, Flo asked Robert if he would like a lesson on how to make an apple pie, one of her specialties. Of course, he was always up for a challenge. There are few desserts that top a home-made apple pie, especially one with a flaky crust. As a bonus, Mr. X would get to enjoy the apple peelings. Robert's first pie was terrific, and for years his pies were such a hit that they became one of his signature delights. Everywhere we traveled—and we traveled together a lot those days—Robert would usually make an apple pie. As a rule, I stayed in the homes of my garden host or hostess. If Robert was invited to stay with me when we traveled, the first thing we'd do when we got into town was shop for apples and other pie supplies. He would then ask my hosts if they would like him to make an apple pie. No one ever said no! The pies were always a hit!

Honesdale, Pennsylvania, was Robert's hometown and numerous relatives and friends stopped by, wanting to get to know Mr. X. As you can tell by now, Mr. X was completely at ease with people and seemed to enjoy all the attention. He even enjoyed being rolled along on Flo's walker while sitting on the cholla!

40 Go with the Flo

So who was having more fun, Aunt Flo or Mr. X?

Chapter 7

New York City, New York

Soon it was time to go back to New York City and the meeting with my editor. We stayed at the famous Algonquin Hotel, where, during the 1920s and '30s, a literary group known as "The Round Table" met daily for lunch.

Members of this august gathering included poet, critic, and screenwriter Dorothy Parker; literary critic, actor, and author (and self-appointed leader of The Round Table) Alexander Woolcott; playwright/ journalist George S. Kaufman; and the irrepressible Harpo Marx.

Here we are in front of the venerable Algonquin Hotel near Times Square

New York City 43

The Algonquin Hotel's famous cat - a hotel tradition

To this day, many publishers put up their authors at the hotel. In addition, the Algonquin is historically pet-friendly, and Mr. X even got to hobnob with their distinguished resident lobby cat.

When we drove into Manhattan at mid-day, it was like a ghost town, with New Yorkers still processing the aftermath of 9/11. We parked inside the entrance to the hotel garage, and, being unsure of Mr. X's welcome at the publishing company, we reluctantly left him in the car.

Robert went to find the attendant and ask him to please keep an eye on our rooster. What followed became the theme for the rest of the trip, as the attendant responded: "ROOOOOSS-TER???", his eyes bugging and voice rising in disbelief. Robert smiled and replied unflappably: "Yes, for two days, please."

Once he was convinced that Robert was serious, the attendant immediately had to meet our feathered companion. As we approached the car, Mr. X crowed a greeting, and out of the depths of the garage we heard two other people incredulously asking each other: "ROOOOOSSTER??? Did you just hear a rooster?" (And, of course, they also had to come over to investigate.)

As we checked into the hotel, the desk clerk mentioned that Broadway had recently reopened, and that he could get us tickets to just about any show. We not only had our choice of the most popular shows, but great seats for a great price, and chose the 8 o'clock show of Kiss Me Kate, which was fabulous—the cast even came out and thanked us for coming.

On our stroll back to the hotel, we passed the windows of the Good Morning America studio, and I said to Robert, half-jokingly: "I bet if you walked by the studio window tomorrow with Mr. X under your arm, someone would come out and ask you to be on the show."

The next morning, I went off to my meeting, and Robert, ever the extrovert (and never one to pass up an interesting challenge), just happened to saunter casually by the GMA studio window with Mr. X in full view. Sure enough, within seconds, a stagehand came running out calling: "Hey, Buddy! Buddy, do you wanna be on TV???"

Spencer Christian, the Good Morning America weatherman graciously poses with our "famous" Mr. X.

Well, duh!

The cast interviewed Robert in a live broadcast, fascinated by his adventures with Mr. X, and by the story of his unusual trip. The interviewers also asked him to get Mr. X to crow—Robert explained patiently that Mr. X didn't do anything on cue.

At the end of the show, my husband asked if someone would please take a photo of the two of them in the studio, thus this priceless shot!

While I was still in my meeting, Robert left Good Morning America and strolled around Times Square. He'd decided that all those dispirited New Yorkers might like something to smile about, and he was certainly right. Everyone he met just brightened up, many wanting to pet Mr. X and learn about him. And he got to hear many more people exclaim, "ROOOOOSS-TER??? There's a rooster in Times Square?!!"

As he walked back to the hotel, Robert, wanting to document this part of their adventure, asked a passer-by to take their photo, with Times Square as a background.

The dynamic duo poses in Times Square

46 New York City

Chapter 8

Long Island and Beyond

Cris Spindler (on the left), the inspiration behind the iconic and family owned Peconic Herb Farm hosted us for a delightful day.

Next, we were off to Long Island, where I was to give a presentation at the Peconic River Herb Farm in Calverton, NY.

Peconic River Herb Farm
I was one of the first speakers on the program that day, so after my talk on *Cooking From The Garden*, I was free to join Robert and Mr. X at the chili cook-off that was part of the daylong event.

I was particularly interested in tasting the chili recipe that I'd entered from my book, and also to see how it had fared in the judging. I was pleased to see that it had wound up in the top 10, but, as it turned out, it wasn't the human judges who had the last word.

Long Island and Beyond 49

"The Boys" posing for yet another portrait.

By this time, Robert and his feathered sidekick had drawn the usual crowd, and someone suggested that Mr. X should also be a judge. The idea was met with much enthusiasm, so the crew laid out a large plate with many selections in front of him, including my recipe.

People crowded around; Mr. X looked the dishes over and immediately chose my entry. Someone shouted, "Fixed election!" and we had a good laugh. Of course, I secretly knew why this had happened; my recipe included corn, usually frowned on by chili aficionados, but one of our rooster's favorite foods!

Saugerties Garlic Festival

The next day we headed off to the Saugerties Garlic Festival, held a couple of hours upstate near the Hudson River. Before we left Long Island, however, I wanted to stop in Flanders to see the Big Duck, a ferrocement building in the shape of — yes, a big duck — which held a lot of memories for me. (Mr. X, never having met a duck in his life, ventured no opinion on the aesthetics of this structure.)

Originally built in 1931 by farmer Martin Maurer as a shop to sell ducks and duck eggs, the Big Duck was added to the National Register of Historic Places in 1997.

50 Long Island and Beyond

I and the late Pat Reppert, the inspiration behind this first East Coast garlic festival, welcome visitors to the event.

Long Island and Beyond 51

A serenade of it's "I've Gotta Crow," from Peter Pan energized the crowd.

Robert's brother John welcomed us, though I don't think the dogs appreciated the bossy Mr. X.

When I was a child, our family would travel every summer from the Boston area to Long Island to spend a few weeks with our grandmother. My sisters and I would always look forward to a stop at The Big Duck. Not only was it fun to visit, but it also meant we only had another hour or so to go before we got to Grandma's.

Arriving in Saugerties, we settled in with our hostess and were delighted that her converted barn was not only a great place to house Mr. X, but also had originally been part of a chicken farm.

Garlic festivals are always lots of fun and feature great food. Robert enjoyed himself as he mingled with the crowd, Mr. X perched jauntily on his arm (followed, of course, by a chorus of people crying out: "ROOOOOSSTER???")

The festival had a formal stage, and Robert decided to check out the music. The woman who was singing spotted Mr. X and started belting out "I've Gotta Crow" from Peter Pan! The crowd cheered!

The next day we packed up and headed for Lewiston, Maine, to visit Robert's brother John and his wife Kathy. We hadn't gotten together in a few years, so we decided it was time for a lobster feast!

Mr. X had already taught the two large resident dogs who was in charge, but when the lobsters started crawling around the back porch, it was an entirely different story—the crustaceans totally had the upper hand.

They wiggled their antennas menacingly at Mr.X, and as they cornered him, you could just see his bewilderment: "How do I even start to defend myself from these—things?" So now our macho guy learned that there were two critters he couldn't dominate: mother peahens and lobsters!

Cincinnati, Ohio and the Rock and Roll Hall of Fame

Before he and Mr. X headed for Florida, Robert decided to go out of his way to see his good friend, Bruce Allen, who was visiting his mother in Cincinnati. Robert had visited Bruce's mom before, but now the message he sent had her puzzled—he had mentioned that he was bringing along a "Mr. X."

Mrs. Allen hadn't heard anything about our rooster, so she wondered who was this mysterious Mr. X?

Long Island and Beyond 53

She didn't know what to expect, so imagine her reaction when Robert showed up with a rooster under his arm! As she said, she wouldn't have guessed that in a thousand years.

While he was in Cincinnati, he and Bruce visited the Rock and Roll Hall of Fame. Bruce kept Mr. X company in the car while Robert took a quick look around. According to the guys, Mr. X wanted to request "Can't Stop the Rooster," and was miffed that the group Alice in Chains had been snubbed by the Hall of Fame.

Robert was delighted to be able to visit the Rock and Roll Hall of Fame.

Chapter 9

Florida Reunion

After Cincinnati, Robert and Mr. X spent a wonderful few days visiting Aunt Flo again, then the Dynamic Duo were back on the road—this time to visit my mother, who at that point was 92 years old and living in a nursing home in Fort Lauderdale, Florida. I flew in to meet up with the boys and to see my extended family.

The day after we arrived, Robert decided he wanted to take Mr. X to see Mom. After all, she had been there when he hatched, and she'd become attached to her "grand-rooster" during her many visits to us.

When Robert suggested this excursion to my sister Nancy, with whom we were staying, she said with horror: "Absolutely not!." She'd been dealing with the nursing home for a few years, and knew that of all their rules, among the strictest was No Animals!

Nancy was weary of dealing with the head nurse, who was a stickler for the rules. In fact, behind her back this woman was often referred to by the nursing home's residents and staff as "Nurse Ratched" (the tyrant attendant in the novel and film *One Flew over the Cuckoo's Nest*). Nancy didn't want to rock the boat, let alone have to deal with the nasty consequences of angering this surly gatekeeper.

Well, Robert was determined; I remember Nancy asking me in exasperation: "Can't you control your husband?" (A silly question; all the rest of us who knew and loved him thought it was kind of hilarious.)

We headed for the nursing home with Mr. X. Robert went in to reconnoiter, found a couple of nurses' aides, told them the story of Mr. X's hatching, and enlisted their help in sneaking him in to visit Mom. They were totally on board, fully understood the issue, and were tickled to be in on the secret, plotting how to keep Nurse Ratched occupied in the other building while Robert snuck a live rooster into the facility,

Naturally, Mr. X was a big hit. I went into Mom's room first. We chatted for a few minutes and then I told her I had a surprise for her. On cue, Robert came in with Mr. X and my mother just lit up—she was so excited to see my husband and his handsome rooster!

As we were leaving a few hours later, a few of the patients got a glimpse of Mr. X and were absolutely delighted. It was always amazing

Mom gets to see her favorite bird one more time.

how many smiles and much pure joy Mr. X left behind wherever he went. We drove back to Nancy's and had a lovely time with the extended

Looks like Mr. X is saying "whatevah dude."

family, celebrating Mr. X's birthday with pizza and a special birthday card.

While we were there, Robert contacted an old friend who had retired to a condo on Miami Beach. On a whim, they decided to take Mr. X to the beach, much to the delight of the children who gathered around him. He was clearly comfortable being a star.

After a few days, it was time for me to fly home and for Robert to get back on the road. His next destination was Houston, Texas, to visit his cousin Bill.

What rooster doesn't like pizza?

Even though it was November, the weather in Texas was still pleasant, and Bill Gammerdinger was getting ready for a camping trip with a group

58 Florida Reunion

Yet again, Mr. X brings excitement.

of boys called the "Trail Blazers." He genially invited Robert and Mr. X to join them for a few days.

A rousing good time was had by all! The children were fascinated with Mr. X, who took to camping like a natural. He loved all the attention from the boys—perhaps they reminded him of all his young "fans" at home. The outing was a great success for everyone.

Florida Reunion 59

The Trail Blazers watch the magical Mr. X strutting around as if he owns the campground.

Chapter 10

Home at Last

I flew home to California, and within a few days Robert and Mr. X arrived back too. We all fell into our usual routine without missing a beat: Mr. X went into the garage at night and out to the coop in the morning. I couldn't help but wonder at times if he missed all the attention and adventures—just imagine being on the road and famous one day and stuck in a chicken coop the next!

As the weather warmed, the garden surged into bloom, and spring arrived in its full glory, celebrating with tulips, daffodils, and lots of fresh greens. It was clearly time for Mr. X (and me) to get back out into the garden.

Our boy still got lots of attention; the neighborhood children were delighted to see him back and often visited with offerings of strawberry hulls, wilted lettuce, and other goodies, watching with glee as he gobbled them up.

One of the mothers told me that her four-year-old son adored our charismatic rooster so much that when she and her family were bringing home his new baby sister, the boy insisted that—even before they got to their house where his grandmother was waiting eagerly to see her new granddaughter—he just had to show her to Mr. X first.

That May, my friend and landscaping client Catherine Debs put on a garden party to celebrate the release of my latest book, and asked if Robert could bring Mr. X to enliven the event. As the two of them mingled with the partygoers, I could hear the ripple of delight. In fact, it made me nostalgic for the road, as I heard the familiar cry of "ROOOOOSSTER????"

Mr. X outshining even the tulips.

Catherine's party was not Mr. X's first soiree. In fact, he was quite the party animal. Each summer our wonderful neighborhood hosted a Fourth of July block party, for which he would usually join us. Not only did the children enjoy his company, but the adults considered him an essential part of the celebration. Mr. X, ever the gourmet, was loud in appreciation of all the treats that came his way.

Socializing with the fabulous Catherine Debs, a truly exceptional hostess.

Mr. X joins the annual block party.

That pak choi looks delicious.

Home at Last 65

Chapter 11

Albuquerque, New Mexico

The year 2002 went by with lots of home-grown rooster tales, but no big traveling adventures. By August of 2003, however, Robert and I were back on the road—I had a number of lectures to give on the east coast, and Robert was headed to Marfa again, still bent on his crusade to solve the mystery of those darn lights.

This time Mr. X didn't fit into our plans, and for such a popular bird, it was surprisingly difficult to find him a rooster-sitter. Many of our friends opted out, probably remembering times when he'd gamely attacked visiting strangers to protect his "flock."

Finally Robert contacted our old friends Patty and Milt Clauser in Albuquerque, New Mexico (if you'll recall, they'd provided us with the egg from which our boy had hatched) to ask if they would rooster-sit for three months.

They agreed, so Robert drove Mr. X back to his "ancestral home." When the two of them arrived, the Clausers assigned our bird to a coop that already had a ruling rooster—a bird they immediately began to refer to as his "country cousin," or "Cousin" for short.

Of course Mr. X jumped right in and declared that he was now in charge—and to prove it proceeded to beat up Cousin five falls out of five! After this face-off, the battling birds fortunately decided that they could co-exist—after a fashion. Patty wrote: "Cousin spent most of the three months huddled on top of an old table, watching Mr. X wasting all his opportunities with the

Mr. X checks out the scenery on his way to NM.

Cousin sits on the table and contemplates his fate.

ladies. Cousin would occasionally sneak down for some food and water, and then would steal into the coop early to get out of Mr. X's sight." Oh, how relieved that poor bird must have been when his domineering "relative" left!

Fowl Nomenclature

I was well into writing this book before I discovered more about Mr. X's breed. He was a Golden Duckwing Standard Old English Game Fowl, one of the oldest chicken breeds in the world, known for its spirit, longevity, and "gameness,' meaning that it was bred for fighting. (You think?)

According to the University of Illinois Extension website: "The bloodlines of the Game Fowl have been used in [creating] many of our most useful breeds of poultry. For hardiness, vigor, and longevity, no breed of fowl excels the Game."

For centuries, cockfighting was a common sport in many countries. These birds were admired for their courage and indomitable spirit—and of course their beauty!

Mr. X herds the sheep to the far corner of the pen.

Clearly, Mr. X fit the "game fowl" description: he was ready to fight for dominance every time he met another rooster, and let the record show that he won every single time! (Peahens and lobsters were, of course, another matter.)

Ranch Life with Mr. X

Before Robert headed back home, he took Mr. X out to explore the ranch, and introduced him to Patty's sheep. Well, he proceeded to show those woolies who was boss, herding them to the far side of the pen at feeding time so he could have the entire wheelbarrowful of feed to himself. After Robert left, Patty occasionally sent emails to keep us up to date with our rooster's day-to-day activities.

Mr. X stares down some hungry sheep.

In a note dated August 12th: "Mr. X is crowing away and seems to enjoy his audience. For their part the hens are laying more eggs." On the 25th, Patty wrote, "Mr. X attacked me and I came back and dumped a bucket of water on his head to teach him to back off. It seemed to work—but only for a few days."

68 Albuquerque

A few weeks later, we received an unsettling note from Patty: she reported that Mr. X must have eaten some deadly nightshade weed— she found him stumbling around and very weak. (She had called a couple of vets and ascertained that the symptoms were not those of West Nile virus.)

She then suggested, tongue-in-cheek, that Cousin might have sneakily egged the hens along to tell Mr. X to eat that tasty weed in the corner, hoping he would do so and succumb to its noxious effects. But not our Super Chicken!

Although he was still falling occasionally when Robert arrived to pick him up, we gave him lots of tender care back home, and he recovered both balance and attitude. (But as an unwanted bonus, Super Chicken arrived home with poultry lice!)

Over the next few years, we took some mini-trips with Mr. X, exploring the eastern side of the Sierras, Hoover Dam, and Yosemite National Park. During that time, Mr. X and Robert—ever the showmen—were featured on a local TV news program.

Mr. X doesn't seem too impressed with Hoover Damn.

Cameraman from a local TV station getting his close up of the "star."

Chapter 12

An Unexpected Goodbye

Life can throw us some terrible curves from time to time, and 2005 was that year for me. In August, my dear Robert was killed in a motorcycle accident.

Our grieving family traveled to the Gold Country, where Robert had been staying, to gather up his belongings and take care of funeral plans, and then headed home.

Because Robert had been away so often on his travels, Mr. X didn't seem to act much differently in his absence. The only sign that he missed his beloved friend came one day when we happened to put some of Robert's soiled clothes in the garage near the nighttime cage: Mr. X made a series of very unusual chortling/gurgling sounds throughout that evening, and from that point on, he seemed to realize somehow that I was now his main "people."

A few weeks later, we held a memorial gathering, and of course, Mr. X was included. As I gave my tribute to my beloved Robert, I held his dear rooster friend close for comfort.

A side note: Years earlier, Robert and I were relaxing on vacation. He'd brought along some CDs, including Pink Floyd's *The Dark Side of the Moon*. As it was playing, Robert suggested that when we died, we should meet on the *The Dark Side of the Moon* and I agreed. It was somewhat comforting to think that, instead of wandering around the universe, we could meet up some day.

Chapter 13

A Birthday Bash

Life went on. Mr. X was now in his 12th year, a very respectable age for any rooster. One day I decided that it would be fun to give him a surprise birthday bash, and immediately went into long-range party-planning mode.

That spring, I had some of the neighborhood children plant a patch of corn that would ripen in September. The children were about five and six years old—the perfect ages for such a fantastical idea. We all agreed it was going to be a surprise, and that we had to keep the secret until the big event. Throughout the summer, the children would come over to check on the corn, and I was amused to see how careful they were to whisper when they were around the coop so Mr. X wouldn't hear them.

In August, I reached out to a few dozen friends and neighbors, inviting them to a corn-themed surprise birthday party for Mr. X. Most everyone RSVPed enthusiastically—as one of my friends wrote: "What a hoot! Wouldn't miss it!"

The day before the party, my crew and I draped a sheet over the front of Mr. X's coop so he couldn't see us decorating the garden. The children whispered and giggled gleefully as they threw colored streamers over the corn and arbors; helped put chairs around to create seating areas; made paper headbands for the guests; and gathered a container full of rooster feathers so each guest could attach one to a headband.

The neighborhood children delight in decorating the corn with streamers.

The big day finally arrived. Out in the driveway was a check-in table where folks could put their name on a headband and choose a feather to attach. Jody Main, another of my talented gardeners, helped the kids harvest and shuck the corn.

As a party is hardly a party without music, I asked our neighborhood disc jockey, the talented Scotty Stanfield, to provide our soundtrack (no chicken music, but lots of oldies).

As a final touch, I'd ordered a special rooster-safe birthday carrot cake with a large rooster cookie in the middle and extra rooster cookies for the crowd. The bakery people were absolutely on board; they could hardly believe that someone would give a surprise birthday party for a chicken, and thought it was hilarious.

Scotty Stanfield sets up the music playbill.

My fabulous gardener Jody Main shows the children how to shuck corn.

The local Draeger's bakery department created a festive carrot cake for Mr. X and my editor Cathy Barash.

Eric Eng masters shucking corn.

The kids were so excited to unveil the coop and let Mr. X join the party. Everyone gathered around, and as I removed the sheet with a great flourish, we all joined in on a spirited rendition of "Happy Birthday Mr. X!" He responded with a loud crow, not a bit disturbed by being the center of attention—his normal comfort zone.

Let the party begin! Scotty started the music and I let Mr. X out to mingle with all his guests. Although he and I knew everyone who was there, many of the guests didn't know each other, but probably had heard of the others. Everyone had a great time tracing their "six degrees of separation" through Mr. X, and the headbands were also great icebreakers.

Long time friend Daniel Hawthorne carefully balances the platter of garden fresh corn.

Friends created these fancy deviled eggs provided by our hens.

Oh, the suspense as I begin to reveal his party to Mr. X.

That afternoon we set up a bar across from the coop, and got ready for our guests. The designated chefs got to cooking for the main event—corn and corned beef were the theme and main dishes.

A Birthday Bash 77

Finally, after months of planning the party has begun.

Even though I had specified on the invitations that no gifts were necessary, a few rooster fans showed up with offerings. (Two favorites were a box of live crickets and a packet of sunflower seeds.) During the celebration, guests had a blast sharing their Mr. X stories, and a great time was had by all—especially by the rooster of the hour, who schmoozed happily with his many admirers.

Cathy's birthday overlaps with Mr. X's so she did the honors and blew out their candles.

A Birthday Bash 79

Chapter 14

Mr. X Takes a Bath

2005 had seen the beginning of a battle (and I do mean battle!) to control Mr. X's New Mexico-acquired lice infestation (Or, as I sometimes thought of it, "Cousin's Revenge.") As a young rooster, he'd been able to stretch his neck to reach his back, but by this time, he'd grown less flexible with age and could no longer control the little buggers on his own.

I'd also recently begun to notice that Mr. X's age was beginning to catch up with him; he was visibly starting to slow down and showing signs of arthritis. After all, at 12 years old he was now a senior citizen (the average rooster's lifespan is eight to ten years).

At first my gardener Rayne MacGeorge and I tried treating him with diatomaceous-earth dust (the fossilized remains of tiny, aquatic organisms called diatoms). This powdery substance was supposed to cause the lice to dry out and die by absorbing the oils and fats from the cuticles of their exoskeletons.

Mr. X was not at all happy with this procedure, during which I had to hold him tightly while Rayne applied the dust under his feathers. He made his objections known as only an annoyed rooster can. And after all that, it didn't work!

Rayne MacGeorge and his favorite rooster.

Mr. X was patient while I held him and Rayne administered the diatomaceous earth dust to control the lice.

Debbie Stern gently held Mr. X in the water to drown the numerous lice.

After a few months, we upped the ante and tried pyrethrum powder—a natural insecticide made from the dried flowerheads of several Chrysanthemum species—again, to no avail.

Then another gardener (Debbie) and I tried a new tactic—chicken bathing! We started by putting Mr. X in an empty tub and slowly adding tepid water to it, all the while offering him brown rice to mollify him. We added a little water at a time, first up to his legs, then a bit deeper, until it reached just below his beak.

He clearly didn't like it, but didn't freak out. You've heard the old saying "Madder then a wet hen?" Well, fortunately that didn't apply to our soggy rooster, who was much more chill under the circumstances than we'd expected.

We were less chill when we saw dozens and dozens of lice appearing in the water. The more we ruffled Mr. X's feathers, the more lice emerged. (Needless to say, this was not a procedure for the faint of heart or weak of stomach.)

After his bath, we took our newly de-loused bird outside to dry off in the sun for a while. An hour or so later, apparently refreshed by his ablutions, he started to strut around and look for critters in the dirt as usual.

I decided at this point, however, that I needed more help with Mr. X's health problems, as he had other issues in addition to the lice. As mentioned, he was slowing down, and his legs seemed to be getting weak. He was also acting a bit listless—not his old feisty self. I needed to find a veterinarian who could help us out.

There aren't too many vets who specialize in the care of birds—let alone roosters—but eventually

A very soggy Mr. X drys out in the sun.

82 Mr. X Takes a Bath

I found a vet hospital called "For the Birds" in San Jose, and made an appointment with Dr. Laura Bellingham, DVM.

Laura seemed to be very comfortable with Mr. X, and he was quite docile with her. She diagnosed a slight heart arrhythmia, poultry lice (still!) and mites. She treated him for the critters, gave him some acetaminophen, and clipped his spurs as well. He stayed there for the afternoon, and by the time we left, he'd perked up, and seemed peppier. Laura said that he probably had been in some pain.

When I got him home, we had to take his crate apart and sterilize it with bleach. I gave Mr. X acetaminophen in some melon and kept him in quarantine for a day so we could sterilize the coop and treat the hens as well.

What an ordeal! Cleaning the coop meant clearing everything out, including the straw and nesting boxes. Then we washed everything down and sprayed it all with orange oil to safely eliminate the pests. It was lucky for Mr. X that we loved him enough to muck around for hours with bleach and chicken poop!

Mr. X was not feeling his best as he sits in the garden.

Chapter 15

Slowing Down

By 2008, Mr. X was really feeling his age. With winter approaching and the temperature in the 40s for days at a time, it was too cold for him to go outside, so I moved his crate from the garage to a warm spot on the kitchen table, where he could be entertained and babied.

At this point, I always kept some type of juicy fruit around to keep him hydrated, because he seemed to be having problems drinking. It was easier to entice him to eat cut-up tomatoes, strawberries, persimmons, and other fruit than to get him to drink water. The seeds from a fresh cantaloupe were one of his favorite snacks, especially if they still had a bit of melon clinging to them.

Mr. X warms himself in front of the fire.

Instead of always buying fresh cantaloupes (I couldn't eat that much melon at one time), I found that I could scoop out seeds and make little packets of them to freeze for the winter. The packets thawed quickly and each was, to Mr. X, as good as fresh! This was also a good way to get his medication into him.

As the year progressed, Mr. X became more fragile; he was still having trouble walking, and by early winter, unlike the gregarious bird that he'd been, sometimes he'd just sit in the coop for hours. It was clearly time to visit For the Birds again.

Cathy Barash and Kate Eng shuck beans and keep Mr. X company.

This time they said that his heart was beating more slowly and not very strongly, so they treat-

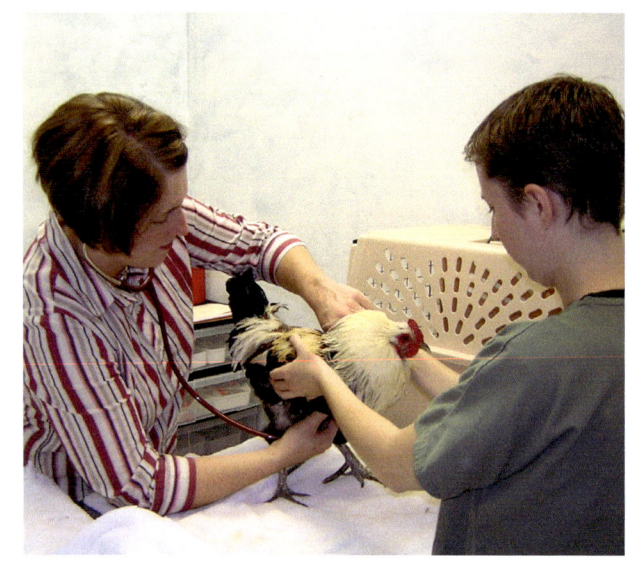

Christmas was approaching and Mr. X was continuing to get weaker and wobbly on his feet. A big decision had to be made: Was he well enough to travel to Marcie and Dan's in San Luis Obispo for Christmas? Did I take him with me, stay home alone (with him as my only company), or—heaven forbid—have him put down?

I discussed my options with two of my neighbors, Kris Stanfield and Katie Bodkin, and both of them said, "When he's ready, you'll know."

Dr. Laura Bellingham DVM examines Mr. X.

ed him with atropine. He spent most of the day sitting, so they rehydrated him again that evening, and had him spend the night there.

The next day, they decided to give him a little digitalis and keep rehydrating him for a while. Finally they said I could bring him home, where he'd be comfortable, and where I could administer the medication to keep him going. "He doesn't seem to be in a lot of pain," they told me, "He's just slowing down."

Mr. X could still stare down Hope the poodle.

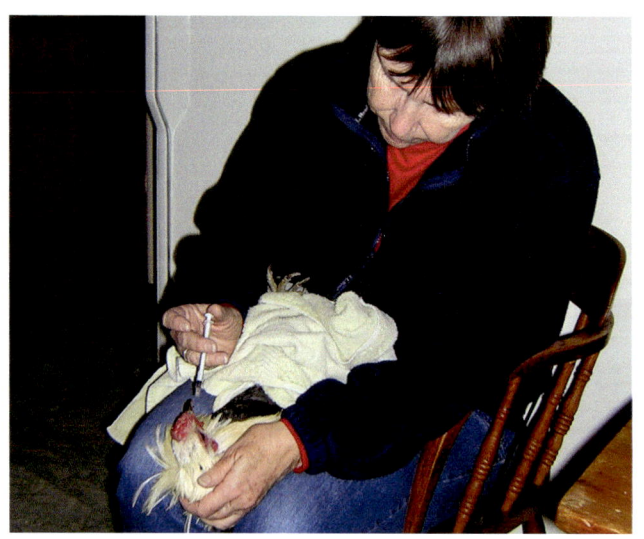

Dear friend Marcy Hawthorne assembles wax paper packets of melon seeds.

Sometimes I needed to actually administer his medications with a dropper.

86 Slowing Down

Mr. X was definitely getting weaker.

My gut said he wasn't ready (nor was I), so I decided to take him with me.

As it turned out, the visit to my friends' wonderful garden—plus all the loving attention—gave him a boost. We took the time to help him walk around the beds and look for critters, always one of his favorite activities.

Once we returned home, Mr. X's routine continued: Time on the kitchen table and an occasional stroll around the garden. As the weather warmed, he also enjoyed sitting in the sun with his "girls" in the chicken coop.

Of course, some days were better than others, but looking back, I'd made a good decision; as the days got longer and warmer, he perked up and would still follow me around the garden. His many medications were obviously keeping him comfortable.

I was blessed to have so many friends that pitched in to keep Mr. X happy and active. Some days, visitors coaxed him to move and helped him walk. The neighborhood children would visit and bring him treats. But my best help was from my editor, Cathy Barash, who was staying with me to help me to update my 1982 book *Edible Landscaping*.

Cathy is a devoted animal lover, and she was especially partial to Mr. X. Day after day they would sit together as she worked at the kitchen table, and most mornings they'd go out to the

Noah and Sierra Hawthorne gently helped Mr. X walk around a bit.

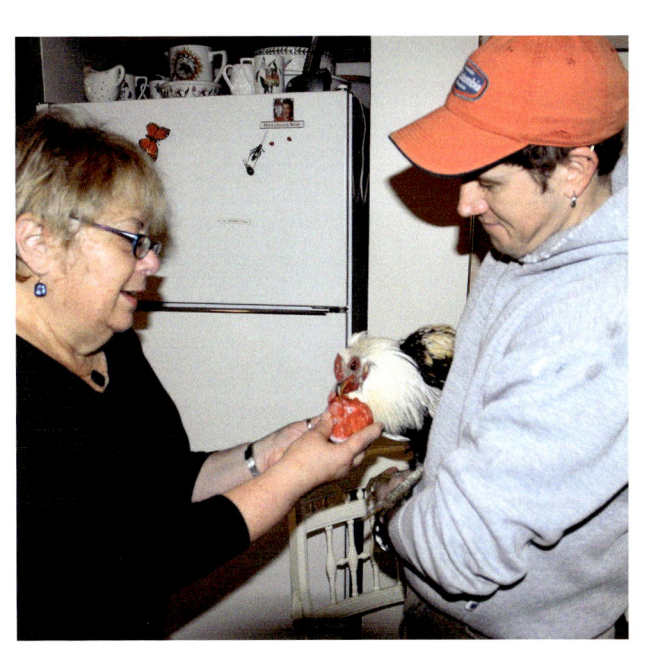

Cathy Barash and Rayne MacGeorge entice Mr. X to eat some tomato.

Slowing Down 87

front porch for breakfast. She'd offer him a spoonful of her oatmeal and he would obligingly pick out the blueberries and sunflower seeds. They made a sweet couple.

On December 19th, 2009, I sent out an email to Mr. X's many friends and fans:

"Mr. X has been slowing down in the last few weeks. He's having more problems walking, and has been sitting in the coop off and on much of his day. This morning he had trouble standing. I brought him into the kitchen and he wobbled around for a while, eating brown rice that I sprinkled around on the floor to encourage him to move. But then he just wanted to sit and he was having trouble getting his legs under him."

"By 9:00 a.m. I was worried enough to take him to the vet again, where he stayed all day and night. They said he was dehydrated, treated him for that and gave him a shot of atropine. He started eating a little, but basically spent most of the day sitting."

"They rehydrated him again this evening and we'll see how he is in the morning. One possibility they suggested was to give him a little digitalis and keep rehydrating for a while. They said I could bring him home tomorrow and keep up the treatment to keep him going. As the vet says, he doesn't seem to be in a lot of pain now, he's just slowing down."

I found these notes in my Palm Pilot dated 1/10/2009:

"Wow, did I make the right decision or what? Mr. X now religiously gets 3ccs of the anti-inflammatory meloxicam™ every afternoon when I bring him inside. It's saved his life! Looking back, he obviously was in pain and made an effort to keep going. Such a noble creature!"

"We now have a new routine: every afternoon I put drops of his medication on small cubes of bread and hold the bowl until he eats every bite. I then either cut up grapes or a large piece of melon for him to keep him hydrated."

"Laundering the non-skid rugs in his crate every day or so, not to mention my clothes, all the hand-sanitizing, cleaning his crate, and washing the bowls for morning and evening—yikes! Who knew that the care and feeding of a geriatric rooster would be so labor-intensive? But, you know, I wouldn't have traded it for anything. This little guy has enriched all our lives so much that he deserves every second of my care."

A few months before he passed Mr. X enjoyed a little time in the garden.

Chapter 16

Crossing the Rainbow Bridge

All went well for the next 10 months, with the medications and care enabling Mr. X to enjoy his "golden years." Then, on Nov 14th, 2009, our wonderful adventure finally ended. Here is the e-mail I sent out to all his fans on the 15th:

"Hi Folks,

A little light went out on our lane this morning. We all knew it was coming, 14 years is a long time for a rooster to live. Last week Mr. X had a hard time walking and seemed sluggish. I took him to the vet, and while most of his vital signs were good, his heart was noisy. They upped his anti-inflammatory medication and I had hopes he would bounce back like he did last Christmas.

On Wednesday he didn't crow in the morning—a first—and when he tried to walk he would fall backwards. On Thursday, when I took him out to walk around on the grass he did let out a few weak cock-a-doodle-doos. Friday seemed a little better too, but he wasn't eating well and seemed quite uncomfortable trying to settle into his crate. We went to bed still hopeful.

Saturday morning the inevitable happened: Mr. X went off to his reunion with Robert on the Dark Side of the Moon! [My editor] Cathy got up early to get ready for her flight home and came and told me. We had a really good cry and then we did what adults do—we got ready for her trip to the airport. Later, I took Mr. X's body to the vet to have him cremated so I could spread his ashes over Robert's grave that summer.

The house feels pretty empty now, but strangely peaceful. Always the gentleman, Mr. X spared me the hard decision, and fortunately he didn't have to suffer too long."

I'd like to share with you a few of the wonderful email responses that I received to the above notice:

- "I held it together on the flight home. But when I stopped to get some groceries, I saw melons and was picking one out for Mr. X until I snapped back to reality…just realizing how much of a surrogate pet he was for me"—Cathy Barash
- "Fond memories of them driving away on their next adventure was really something. You both embraced him in a most unusual way and taught everyone love and expression for every living being has no boundaries."—Jody Main
- "May he crow in the clouds, rainbows and beautiful edible gardens forevermore. He was indeed more than a mere bird…a muse, amusement, connection to more than mere mortals can ever understand. As I turn over lumps of fresh garden clods and see the worms wiggle, I always think of him and how well he had us humans trained."—Marcie Hawthorne
- "He was one very special rooster, I really loved that bird."—Aunt Flo Gammerdinger
- "Had an incredible life for a chicken and taught a lot of people about humanity."—Kim and Steve Axelrod
- "Like his dad, he was one of a kind."—Bill Gammerdinger
- "What a bird! And what a life that bird had! How many chickens get to go on a "world tour?"—Linda Avery
- "Take comfort that now he is with Robert and they can travel the spirit world together, spreading joy and wonder as they did here."—Glenda Hughes

Epilogue

In the nearly 15 years since Mr. X left us, my friends and family have continued to celebrate his incredible spirit! One of my first memorial gestures was in the form of a custom USPS postage stamp with his portrait on it. I use the stamps on correspondence with friends and family who knew and loved our boy.

My artist friend, Marcie Hawthorne, painted his portrait on my bathroom wall.

Since his death I've had fun collecting rooster garden decorations. They're usually spread among the different parts of the garden, but for fun one day I lined them up for a group photo. Over the years, my friends, relatives, and I have collected numerous rooster-themed items such as kitchen towels, bowls, and earrings.

To commemorate my Dynamic Duo, a friend's nephew, Clark L. Gussin, painted a portrait of Robert and Mr. X. It hangs in a place of honor on my kitchen wall.

In these images, and in the hearts of all of us, this unforgettable and indomitable little bird lives on.

96 Epilogue

Epilogue 97

An arbor festooned with cherry tomato plants welcomes people to Ros's garden. In the bountiful beds are zucchini and collards, a blueberry bush, and a dwarf lemon tree.

Rosalind Creasy is a garden and food writer, photographer, and landscape designer with a passion for beautiful vegetables and fruits, (above, a view of her edible landscape in the front yard) and the conviction that gardening should be an ecologically positive endeavor. For her, that includes chickens.

Rosalind brings an enormous gardener readership and following for this book. Her 42 years of horticultural writing (17 books); giving countless lectures; recording over 20 YouTube videos, and participating in many radio and television interviews have exposed millions to her work. She has sold nearly 500,000 books. Rosalind also wrote a gardening column for the Associated Press through The Los Angeles Times for four years.

Rosalind Creasy is also an accomplished photographer (see above), and her photos have been featured in dozens of books and hundreds of magazine articles.

www.rosalindcreasy.com